O is for

Ownership!

The ABCs of the Stock Market for Beginners

Written By
Leslie Clark

Illustrated By
C.J. Love

Copyright © 2022 by CAMsDEN Publishing, LLC
ISBN: 979-8-9870138-2-3

Illustrations copyright © 2022 by C.J. Love

Published by: CAMsDEN Publishing, LLC
Printed in the United States of America

It is a blessing to be a blessing. I thank God for giving me the vision to share this message of ownership. The only way to truly be free is to take ownership of anything and everything that is a part of your everyday life (including your actions!)

Generational Wealth refers to any kind of asset that families pass down to their children or grandchildren, whether in the form of cash, investment funds, stocks and bonds, properties, or even entire companies.

As witnessed in society today, it is never too early to learn how to be good stewards of your money or make sound decisions to ensure that you are financially stable. Due to a lack of knowledge, many fear the stock market. Hence, there are numerous streams of untapped income. My hope is that this book serves as a catalyst for financial empowerment related to the stock market. Knowledge is power! And money, aha!

There are 3 important things that can be attributed to investing in the stock market

1. Personal Ownership – Owning a stock means buying a percentage of ownership in the company. Ownership is power; it's really the primary path to wealth. Owning real estate, stocks, or your own company is how 85% of people become wealthy. The best part is that it's transferable for generational wealth!

2. Building Wealth – By making conscious decisions about where your money is invested, your money is ultimately working for you!

3. The Health of the Economy – When the stock prices rise, people invested in the equity market gain wealth. This increased wealth often leads to increased consumer spending. As consumers become more confident in their financial situation, they tend to buy more goods and services.

A

Ask

The price at which you are willing to sell a share

B

Bull/Bear Market

Bull: When the stock prices in a market are generally rising
Bear: When the stock prices in the market are generally falling

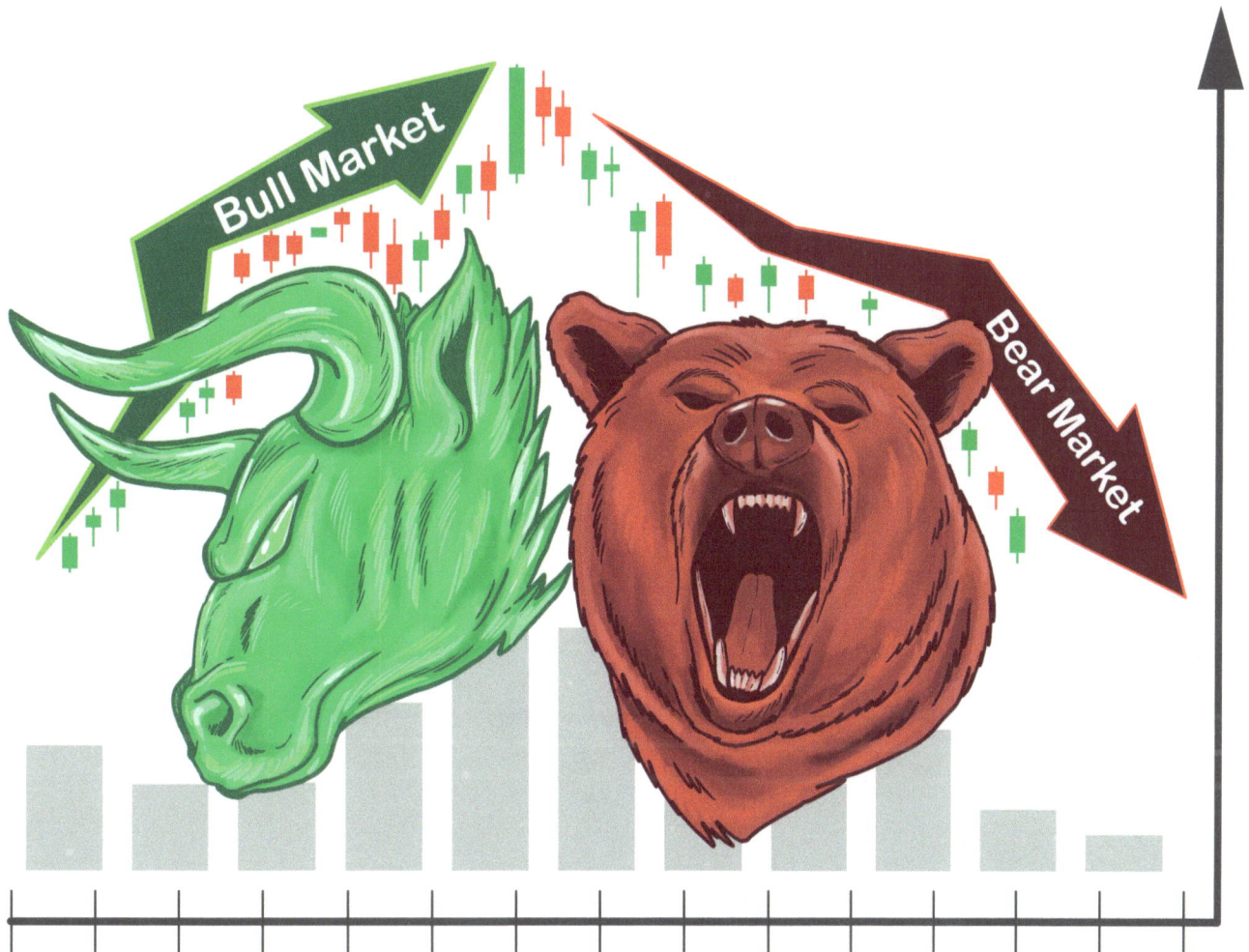

C

Cancel

To void an order to buy or sell from (1) the floor or (2) the trader/salesperson's scope

D

Dividends

Part of the profit distributed by a corporation among its shareholders

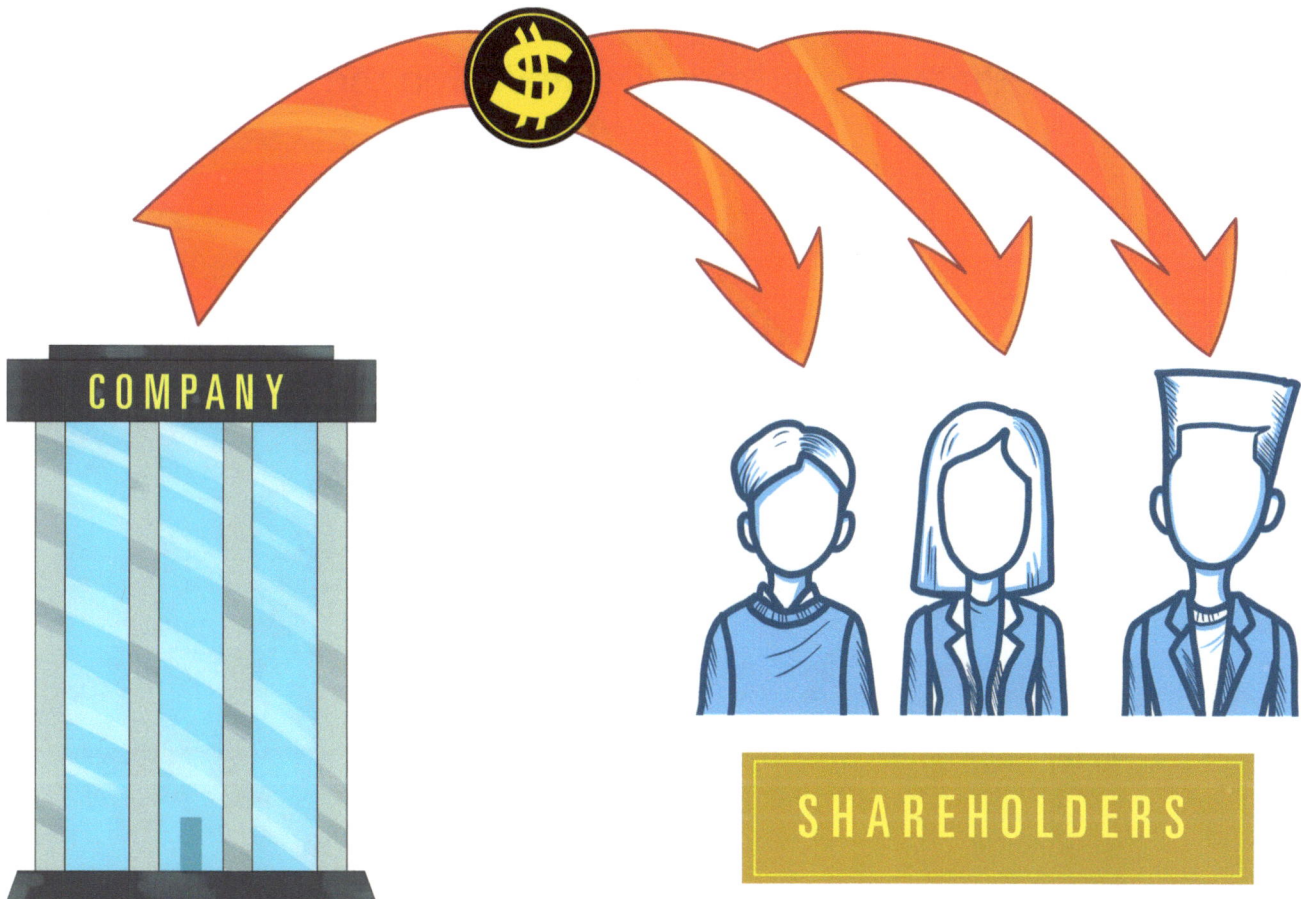

E

Exchange-Traded Funds (ETFs)

Mutual funds that you can trade like shares on the stock exchange

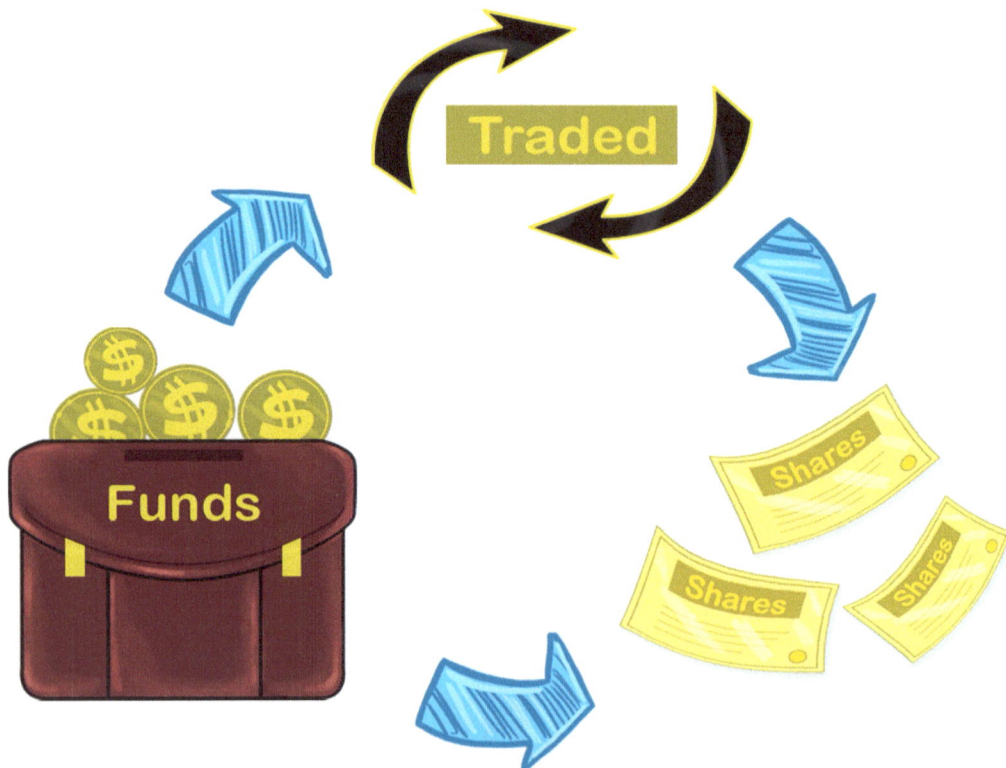

F

Float

The number of shares available to the public (to trade)

G

Going Long/Going Short

Going Long: When going long, you purchase stock shares hoping to profit from an increase in the stock price

Going Short: When a trader tries to profit from a stock's dropping price

H

Hedge

A transaction that reduces the risk of an investment

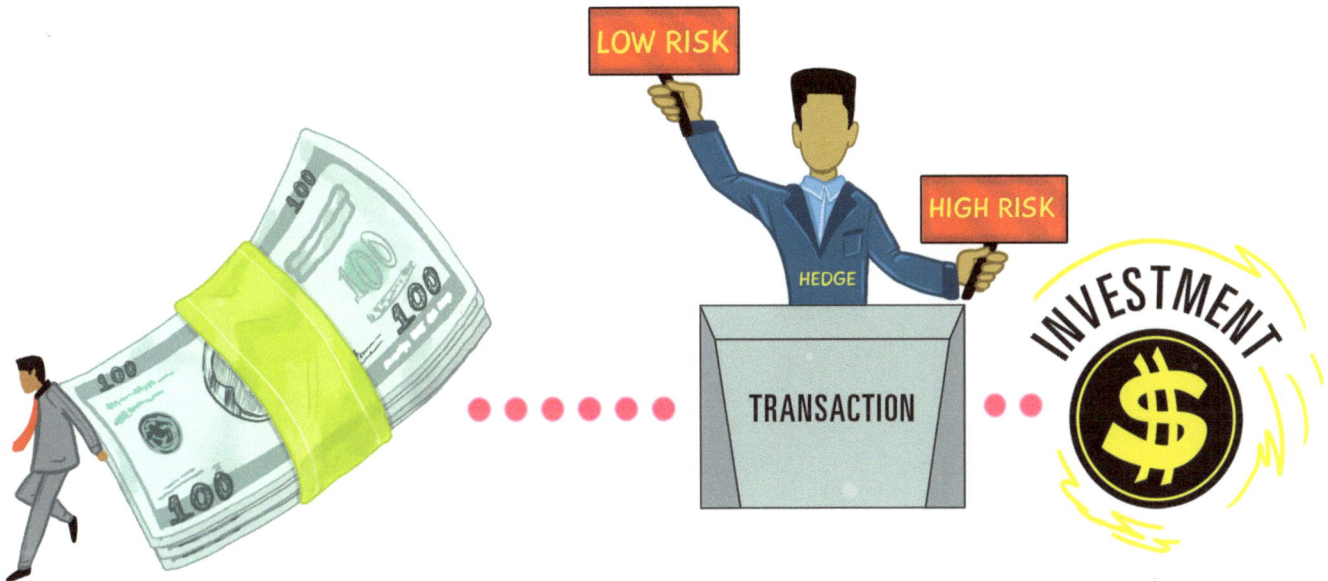

Index

A benchmark that is used by investors and portfolio managers to measure market performance

J

January Effect

Refers to the historical pattern that stock prices rise in the first few days of January

K

K

The letter "K" is one of many NASDAQ ticker symbol extensions that tell investors various things about that particular stock; this letter specifies when the shares offer no voting rights

LIBERTY GLOBAL
NASDAQ: LBTYK :

TICKER SYMBOL
EXTENSION

L

Limit Order

Provides instruction to (1) only execute at or under a purchase price or (2) at or above a sale price

LIMIT (SELL)

MARKET (BUY OR SELL)

LIMIT (BUY)

M

Market Order
An order to sell/buy shares at the market price

N

Nasdaq Stock Market/New York Stock Exchange

NASDAQ: The first electronic stock market listing over 5000 companies. The Nasdaq stock market comprises of two separate markets, namely the Nasdaq National Market, which trades large, active securities and the Nasdaq Small Cap Market that trades emerging growth companies

NYSE: The largest equities-based exchange in the world, based on the total market capitalization of its listed securities

O

Order

A show of intent to buy or sell shares in a given price range

P

Portfolio

The collection of all the investments an investor has made

Q

Quote
A stock's latest trading price

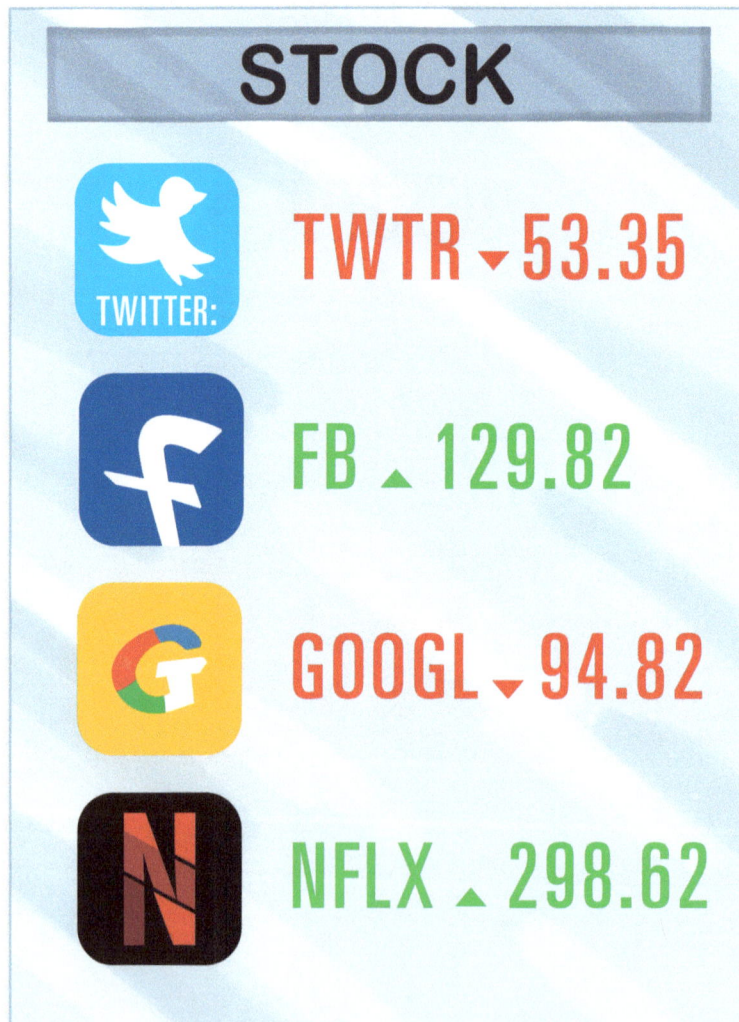

STOCK	
TWITTER:	TWTR ▼ 53.35
FB	FB ▲ 129.82
G	GOOGL ▼ 94.82
N	NFLX ▲ 298.62

R

Rally

A rapid increase in the general price level of the market or of the price of a stock

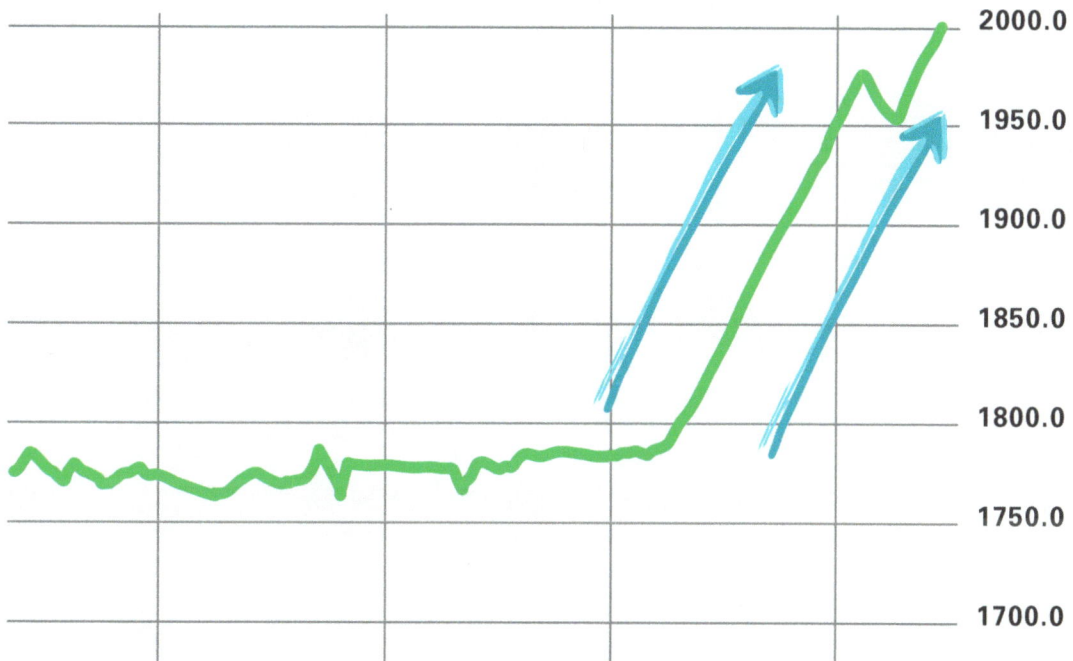

S

Stock/Share

Stock: A general term used to refer to a certificate indicating ownership in a company

Share: A stock certificate of a particular company

T

Trading Volume

The number of shares being traded on a given day

Volume ■

U

Undervalued

A stock price perceived to be low or cheap, as indicated by a particular valuation model

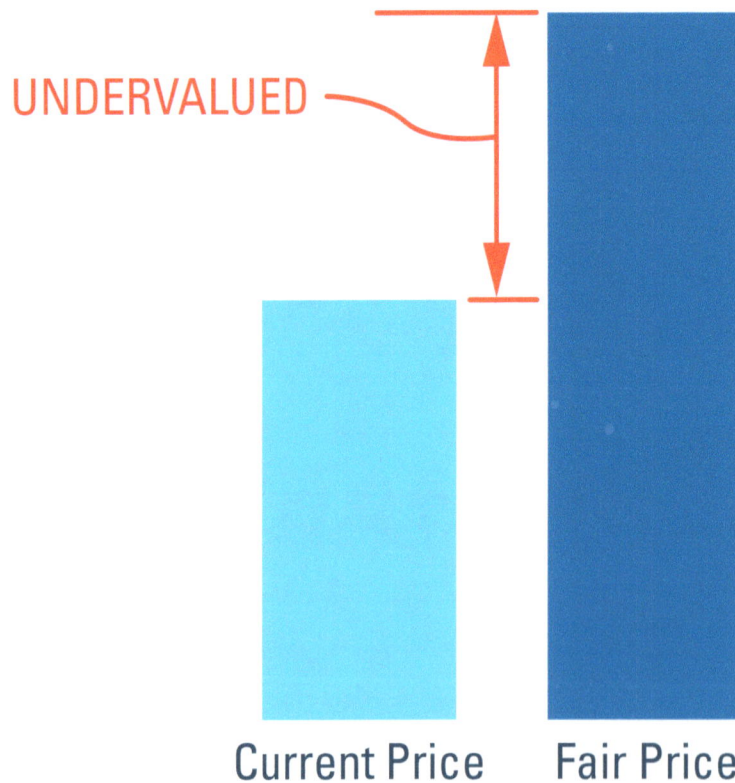

UNDERVALUED

Current Price   Fair Price

STOCK NAME: 🍎 APPLE

V

Volatility

How much and how quickly prices move over a given span of time

W

Wilshire Indexes

Widely followed performance measurement indexes measuring performance of all the US headquartered equity securities with readily available price data, created by Wilshire Associates, Inc.

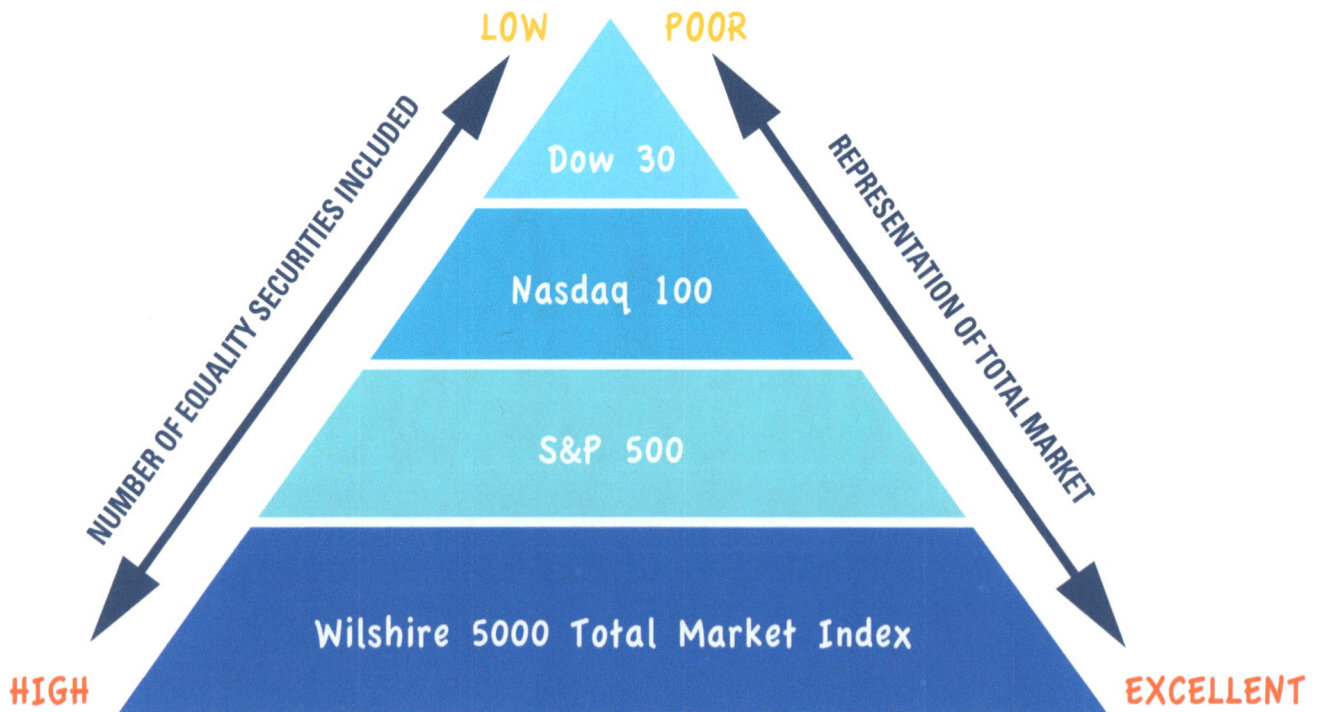

LOW   POOR

NUMBER OF EQUALITY SECURITIES INCLUDED

REPRESENTATION OF TOTAL MARKET

Dow 30

Nasdaq 100

S&P 500

Wilshire 5000 Total Market Index

HIGH

EXCELLENT

X

x

The letter "X" is one of many NASDAQ ticker symbol extensions that tell investors various things about that particular stock; This letter indicates that the listing is a mutual fund

X = MUTUAL FUND

VSMPX

VIGIX

VMCIX

VSCIX

Y

Yield

The measure of the return on an investment that is received from the payment of a dividend

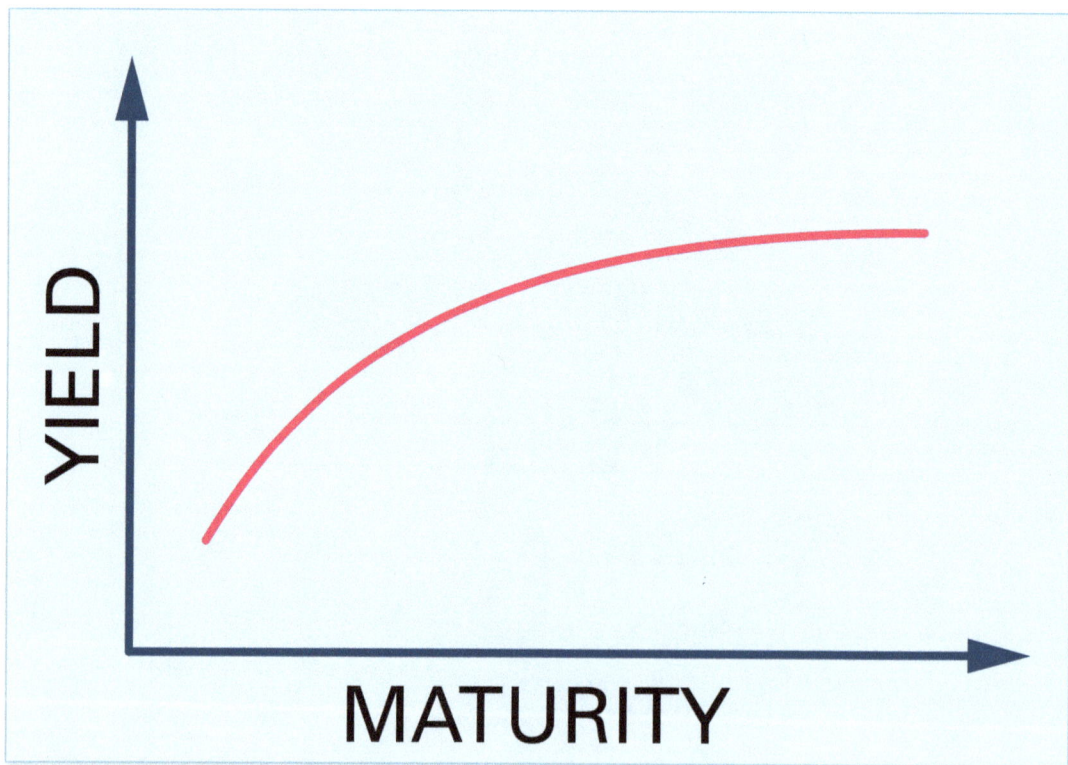

Z

Zone of Resistance

The upper range of a stock's price that shows resistance, with the lower range being its support levels.

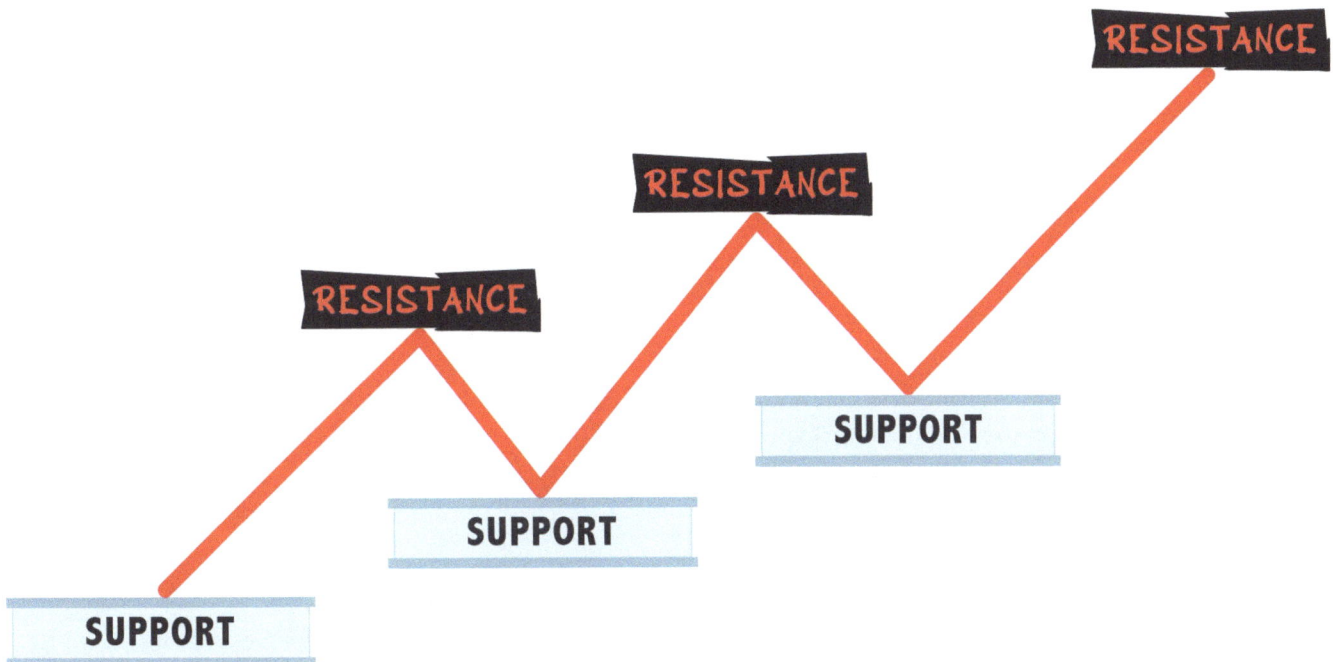

Extended ABCs: Additional terms to assist with learning the Stock Market

- **Bid/Buy/Sell**
    - **Bid** – When a trader in the market makes an offer to buy shares
    - **Buy** – To take a position by buying shares of a company
    - **Sell** – To sell shares you currently own

- **Blue-Chip Stocks** – Represent the biggest companies in the country; they are often some of the safest stocks to invest in

- **Broker** – A firm or person who executes your buy and sell orders for stocks or other securities

- **Cyclical Stocks** – Stocks that respond to economic issues on a seasonal cyclical basis

- **Day Trading** – The practice of entering and entering stock trades within the same trading day, before the close of the markets on that day

- **Growth Stocks** – Stocks that are shares of companies that are growing rapidly and have the potential of generating higher returns on your investment but may come at a higher risk

- **Hedge Funds –** The type of investment fund that often uses non-standard investment and standard techniques

- **Income Stocks –** Stocks that generate most of their returns in dividends, which in many cases grow continuously year after year as the companies' earnings grow

- **Initial Public Offering (IPO) –** When a company goes through the process of selling shares on the stock market for the first time

- **Mutual Funds –** Pools of investor capital for investing in stocks, bonds, and other financial assets

- **Non-Cyclical Stocks –** Stocks that tend to do well in economic downturns, since demand for their products and services continue regardless of the economy

- **Penny Stocks –** Common shares of small public companies that trade at low prices per share

- **Post-Market Trading –** After hours trading that takes place after the markets have closed, typically between 4 p.m. to 8 p.m. EST

- **Pre-Market Trading** – Trading activity that occurs before the regular market session, typically between 8 a.m. and 9:30 a.m. EST each trading day

- **Spread** – The gap between the bid and the ask prices of a security or asset, like a stock, bond, or commodity.

- **Stop Loss** – An order placed to liquidate/sell position when a specified price is reached or passed to stop any further losses

Leslie Clark is a wife, mother, engineer, entrepreneur, and author. Her love for children and volunteering in her community sparked her desire to write books that reflect on issues as well as topics she believed were not being discussed. Clark is a native of Bradenton, Florida but currently resides in Buford, Georgia with her husband and kids. This is the first of many books to come from Clark. She has been jotting down her ideas for over a decade but has recently found the spark needed to turn those ideas into a reality. Her goal is to reach as many children of all backgrounds as she can and instill in them a spirit of love, ownership, and lifelong learning.

Illustrated & Designed By:
C.J. Love
C.love2design@gmail.com
www.clove2design.com

www.ingramcontent.com/pod-product-compliance
Lightning Source LLC
Chambersburg PA
CBHW050912210326

41597CB00002B/99